biomimicry

WHEN NATURE INSPIRES AMAZING INVENTIONS

Séraphine Menu & Emmanuelle Walker

translated by Alyson Waters

biomimicry

WHEN NATURE INSPIRES AMAZING INVENTIONS

SEVEN STORIES
TRIANGLE SQUARE
books for young readers

SEVEN STORIES PRESS
NEW YORK · OAKLAND · LIVERPOOL

Table of Contents

LONG LIVE LIFE!

All around us rich, complex, and diverse nature is constantly evolving, always changing. It can seem messy and unmanageable because human beings try so hard to control it, but in truth everything is well ordered, painstakingly calculated, and extremely organized.

In nature, nothing is left to chance and every tiny detail is significant. From the mosquito to the whale, from the daisy to the baobab tree, the slightest little thing matters. Our life, too, is intimately tied to a multitude of small things that contribute to this fragile balance that must be preserved at all costs.

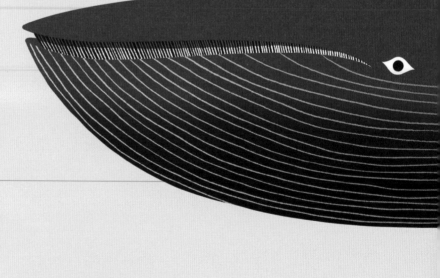

Essential Ecosystems

If we observe how an ant colony or a beehive works, we can immediately understand that nature is amazingly well structured. It's filled with micro-organizations called "ecosystems" that function independently, but also depend on one another. In this way, nature resembles a huge machine: each cog must be in its proper place and mesh with the others.

The oceans, forests, plains, rivers, and savannahs that cover our planet take care of their own regeneration and also participate in its overall equilibrium. Thanks to these ecosystems, the earth is constantly renewed and remains a place that supports life.

And What About Us in All That?

Human beings are also part of this vast machine,
sometimes harmonious, sometimes dangerous.
If we decide to live in harmony with nature,
the planet will allow us to live peacefully.

However, if we exploit the earth's resources and treat it badly, the areas that allow life to prosper will dwindle. When fragile ecosystems like tropical forests or great lakes are harmed, this threatens both the beautiful planet's and our own equilibrium.

Luckily, the people who live on earth are very resourceful and have managed to adapt to changes since the beginning of time. We learn, evolve, and advance as the world turns.

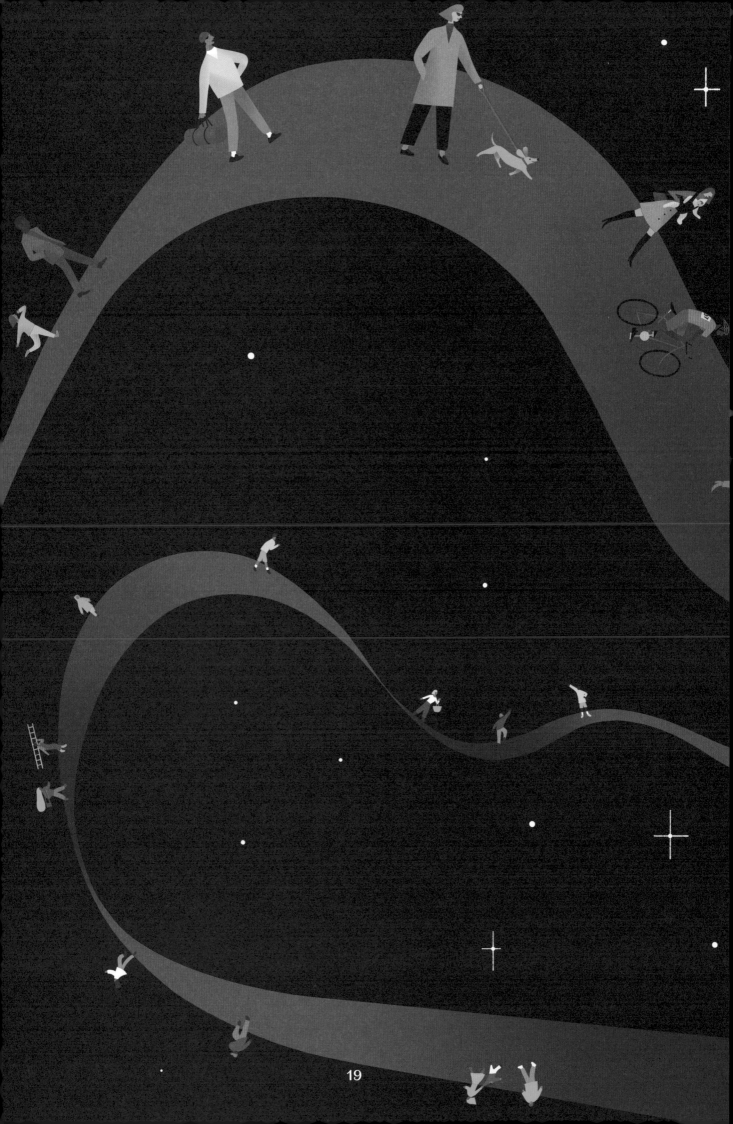

Human beings are capable of creating things
to improve our living conditions. We can also
construct spaces to comfort and protect us.
We create, build, test, and develop things all
the time.

Often, nature accompanies us. It's at the center of our thinking and serves as a model for us. And this is the basis of biomimicry.

"Biomimicry"?

The term "biomimicry" comes from the Greek "bio" (life) and "mimesis" (imitation). It appeared in scientific texts in the 1980s, but the American scientist Janine Benyus was the one who popularized it. In 1997, she published the first book on the subject, in which she discusses a number of innovative projects that rely on observing nature. Since then, biomimicry has been defined as the discipline that studies ecosystems and living organisms in order to apply their solutions and strategies to a human context.

A Bit of History

Whereas the word "biomimicry" is recent, humans have been getting inspiration from nature for ages. Since the earliest times, men and women have looked at how their environment functions and have made use of what they've observed. In antiquity, for example, nature inspired both the arts and the sciences.

Ancient Greeks succeeded in measuring time by looking at the sun's path in the sky. This allowed them to create the first sundials, the precursors of our wristwatches today.

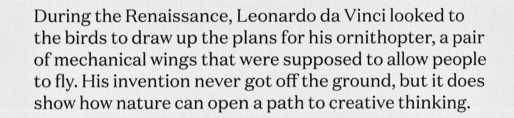

During the Renaissance, Leonardo da Vinci looked to the birds to draw up the plans for his ornithopter, a pair of mechanical wings that were supposed to allow people to fly. His invention never got off the ground, but it does show how nature can open a path to creative thinking.

29

Later, while the great scientist Isaac Newton was watching an apple as it fell from a tree, he realized that things were attracted to the ground by an invisible force, and he developed the first theory of gravity.

So: observation leads to comprehension, which leads to action.

BIOMIMICRY AND SCIENCE

Nature has proved to be an inexhaustible source of inspiration to scientists. It has served as the springboard for countless technical innovations and the basis of so many ingenious ideas.

From Mussels to Glue

Did you know that industrial wood glue and biomedical glue were developed after scientists studied mussels? These mollusks have a remarkable ability to stick to rocks. They can attach themselves so mightily that even ocean currents can't budge them. It was while observing the sticky strings that mussels release in the water that the idea of creating something similar and commercializing it was born.

Adhesive, which belongs to
the same family as glue, was also
developed by observing nature.
For a long time scientists studied
the toe pads of geckos—those little
lizards that can stay stuck to walls
for hours—to create super sticky
adhesive tapes.

From Fireflies to LED Light Bulbs

LED light bulbs, also known as "electroluminescent diodes," have many advantages. They are compact, come in several colors, and consume very little energy. But they do not give off a lot of light.

In order to make LED bulbs shine more brightly, scientists have been examining fireflies. Their abdomens are covered with small zigzagging scales that retain and intensify light.

From the Bat to Radar

Did you ever see a bat fly? It moves swiftly in the dark without bumping into anything. Scientists investigated this ability for a long time. They discovered that the bat uses ultrasound to find its way in space ("echolocation"), and then they developed a similar tool: radar. Radar detects the presence of objects in an area by sending out electromagnetic waves.

From the Bee to Plastic

Some bees don't only make honey. In parts of northern Europe and Asia, there are amazing bees capable of producing plastic. These bees, known as "Collettes," produce a kind of transparent cellophane (like what we use to wrap our food) that they place around their underground nests to protect them. This material is waterproof and very resistant—it safeguards the bees' eggs.

Nowadays plastic is made from petroleum and takes over four hundred years to decompose. This is a serious problem for the environment. Studies have been begun to determine if this natural plastic from bees can serve as the model for an alternative to our non-biodegradable plastics.

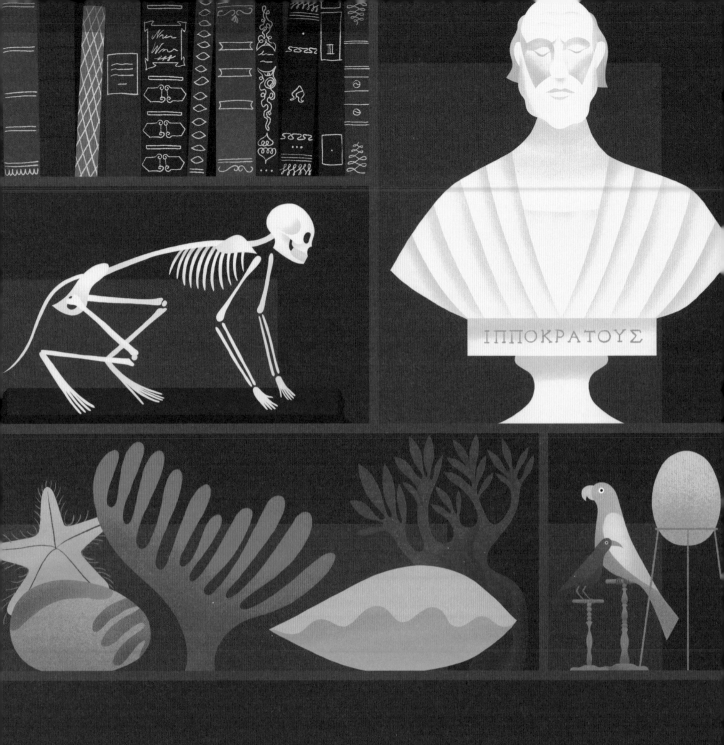

BIOMIMICRY AND MEDICINE

Scientific discoveries lead to medical progress. In this field more than in any other, each step forward directly helps people live better and longer. From what natural phenomena has medicine drawn inspiration?

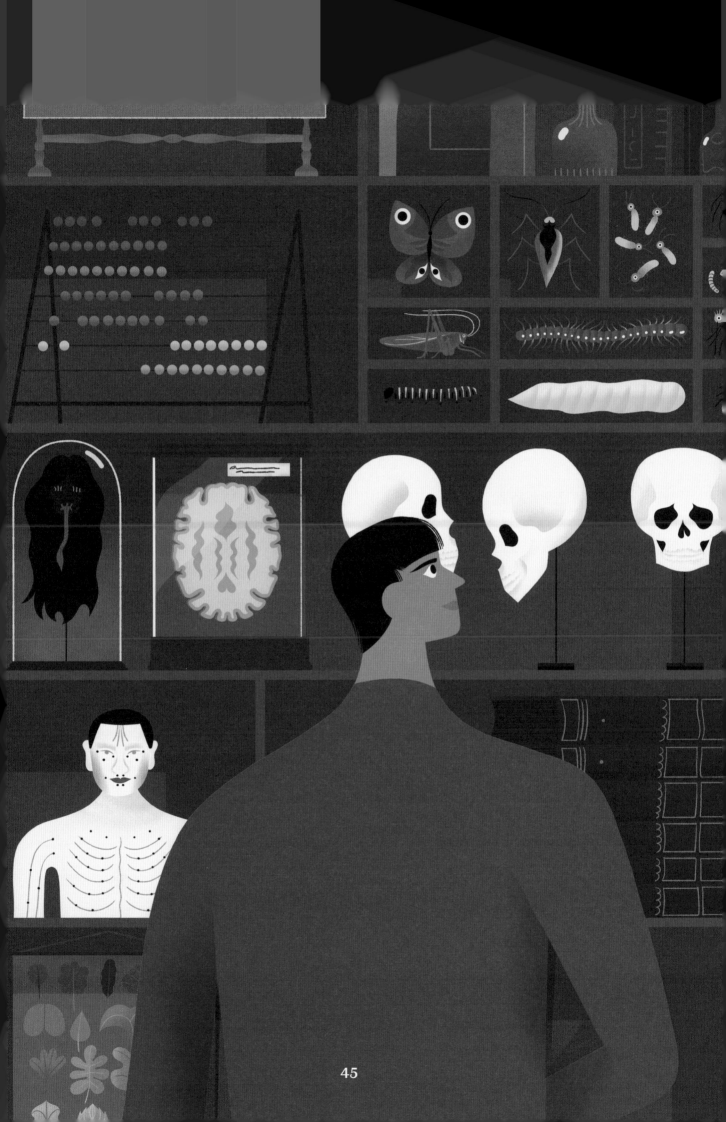

The Heart and Whales

In whales' hearts, blood circulates slowly, at the rate of three to four heartbeats a minute. Small electrical signals are sent at regular intervals to wake up this organ and remind it to do its work. The American scientist Jorge Reynolds Pombo carefully studied how whale hearts function and in 1958 he invented the pacemaker, a cardiac stimulator that works like a tiny battery and restarts the human heart by emitting electrical impulses.

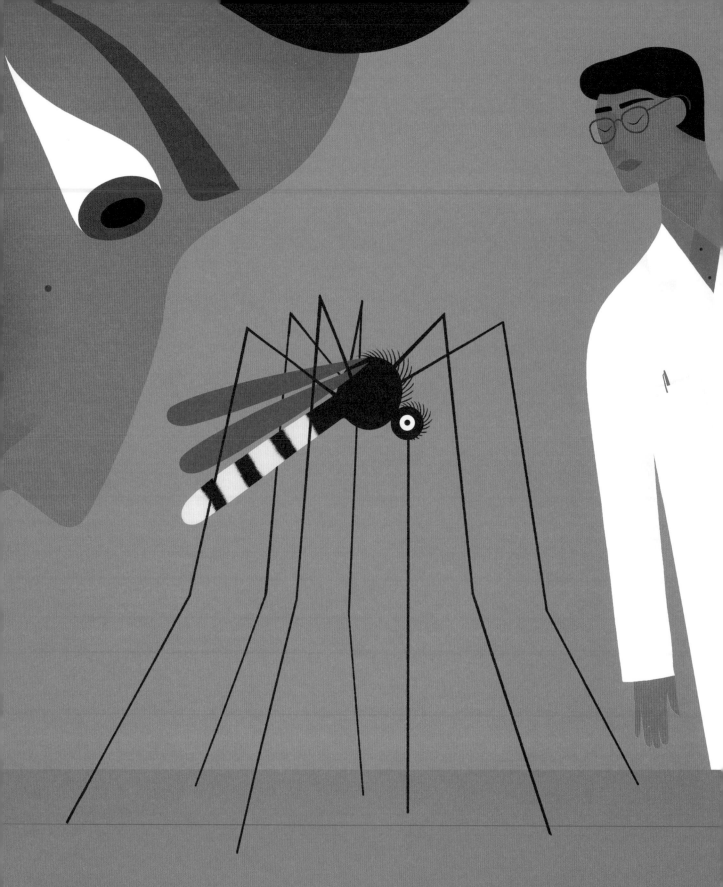

The Mosquito's Proboscis

The bite of the mosquito's straw-like mouth, called a proboscis, is painless. (But it sure itches after!)

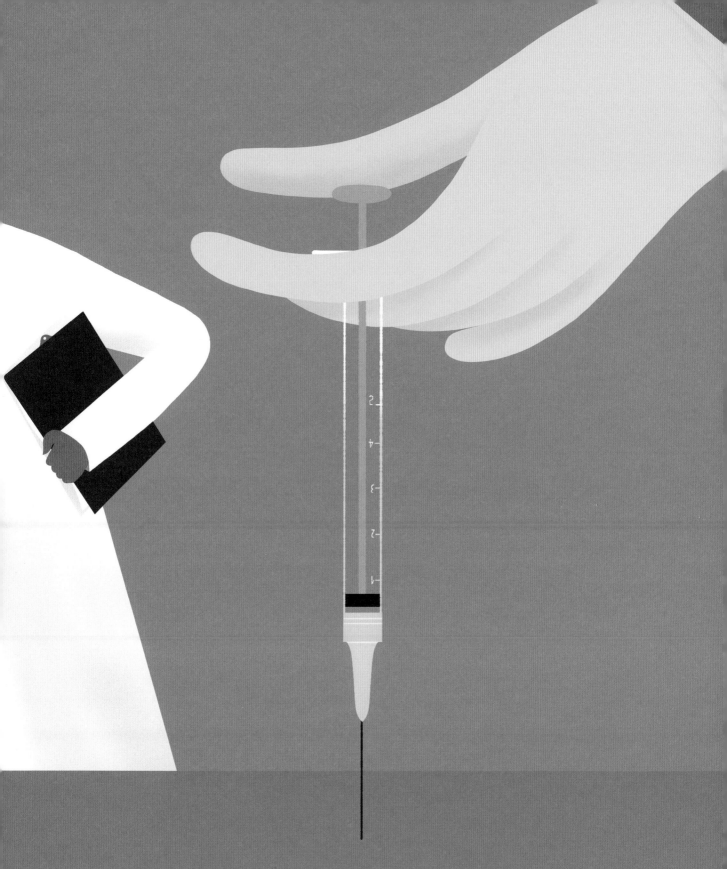

So using the proboscis as a guide, Japanese scientists
have perfected medical needles shaped like cones rather
than like cylinders. If this product hits the market, blood
tests and vaccinations will be practically pain free.

The Nervous System of Invertebrates

Snails, slugs, squids, and shrimps are invertebrates.
They have no bones or spinal columns. But they are
loaded with nerves and have the ability to regenerate
and repair themselves.

This ability has motivated medical science to try to develop similar techniques to repair the human nervous system.

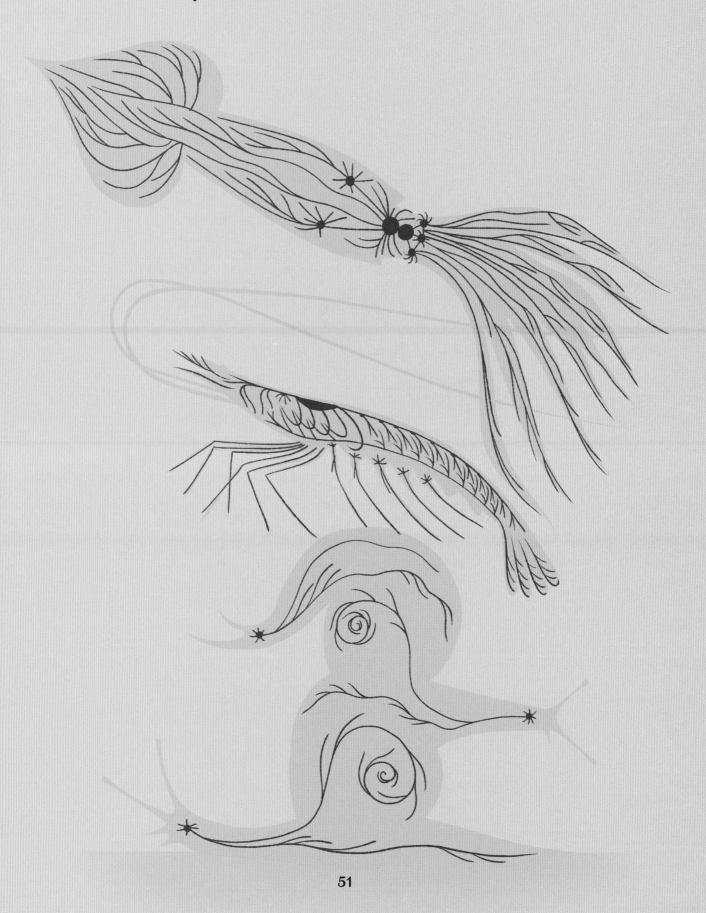

BIOMIMICRY AND OUR CLOTHES

Nature has influenced the clothes we wear, and may continue to do so in the future. Did you know, for example, that Velcro was invented by observing a plant? The burdock, whose flowers stick to fabric, led to the invention of Velcro, a detachable material we find on our clothing today.

The lotus flower has provided the textile industry with several ideas. Drops of water simply roll off of the flower's petals, carrying dust with them. These petals had already served as models for self-cleaning glass and shower walls. Textile manufacturers are studying them carefully, hoping one day to create waterproof fabrics that resist stains and don't wear out.

But that's not all: there are bathing suits and diving suits that imitate sturdy, elastic shark skin.

And spider silk, one of the most resistant
materials in the world, is used to make
bulletproof vests.

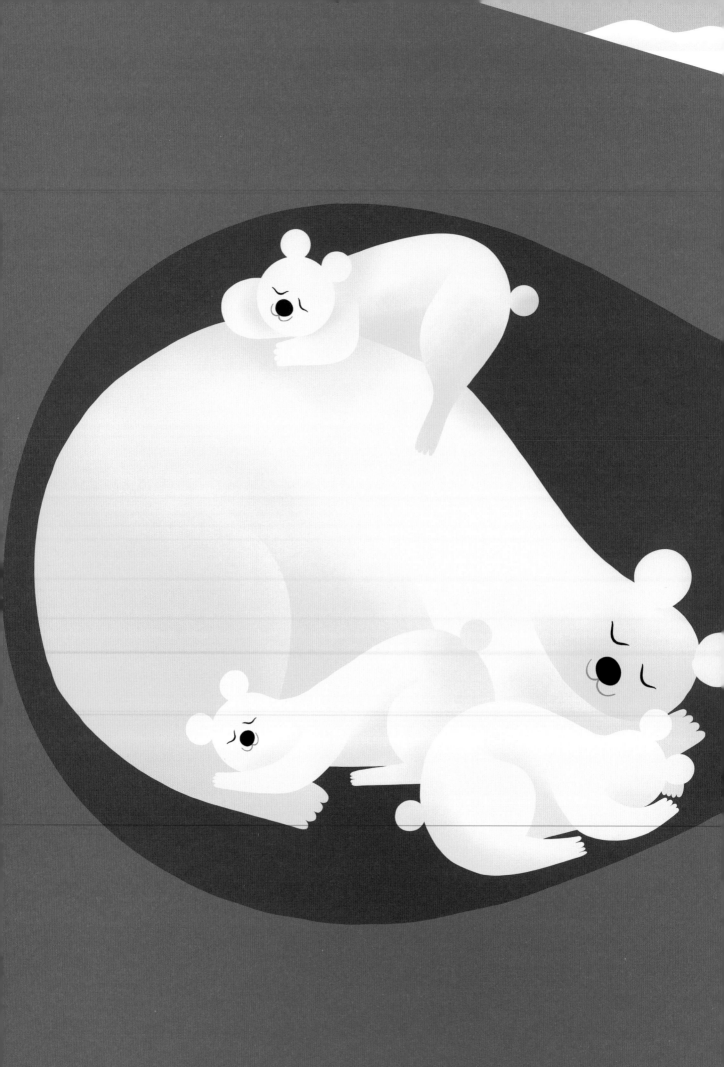

BIOMIMICRY, DESIGN, AND ARCHITECTURE

Ancient Egyptians based the shape of their sanctuaries on the position of sleeping elephants. The Inuit build their igloos based on the polar bear's den. Today architects and designers still look to nature for ideas for new living spaces.

Organic Architecture

The Spanish architect Antoni Gaudí, who designed the Sagrada Familia and the huge Park Güell in Barcelona, was greatly inspired by nature. The facades of his buildings ripple, the walls meander and are covered with scales, and the window frames look like animal bones.

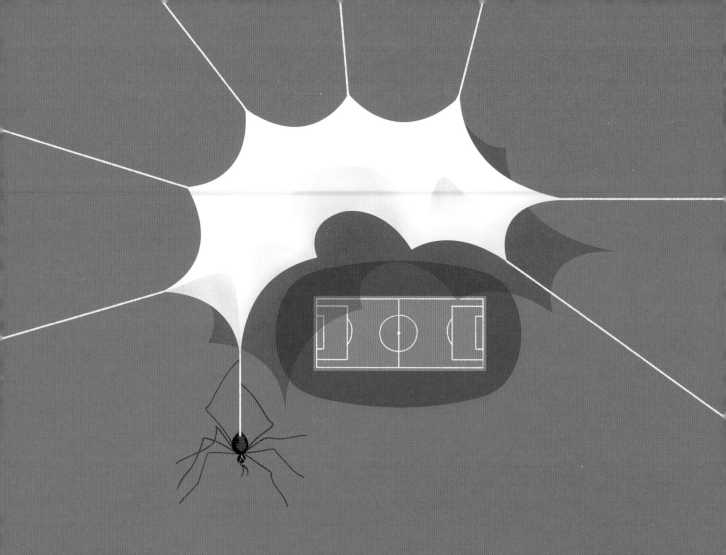

The Olympic Stadium in Munich, Germany, resembles a giant spider web. And the facade of the CH2 building in Melbourne, Australia, imitates tree bark.

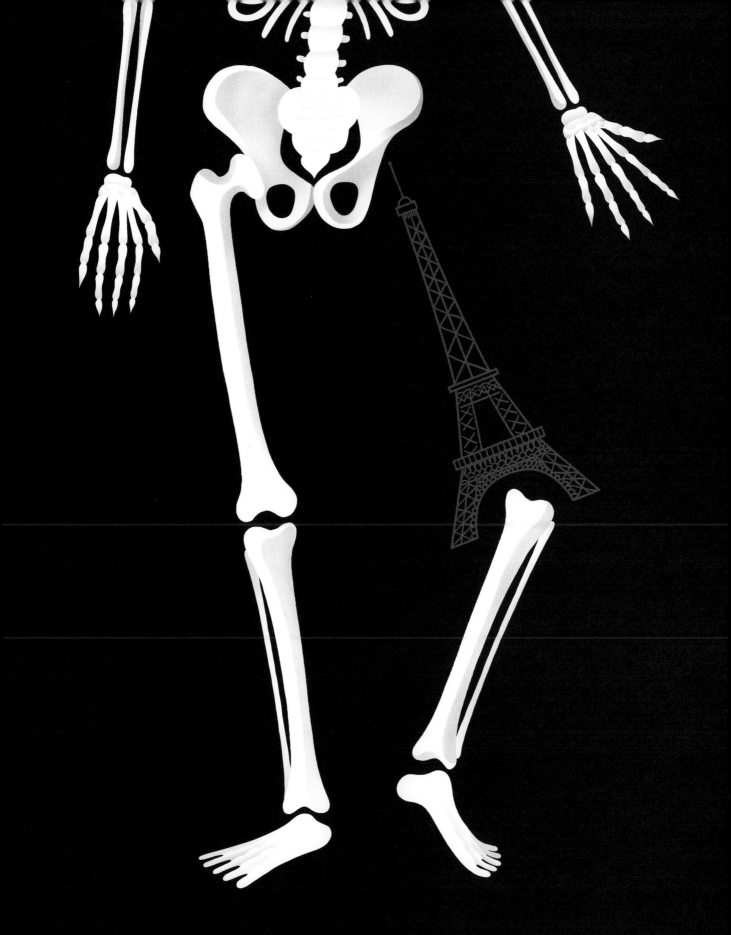

It's even been said that the design of the famous Eiffel Tower in Paris was based on the human femur bone, the toughest bone in the human body.

Eco-Friendly Designs

But architects didn't only look to nature for esthetic reasons. In Zimbabwe there is a remarkable building in the city of Harare that was inspired by termite hills.

Termite hills are small mounds open at the top; they are warmed by the sun and provide shelter to termites. Their inside temperature remains constant, regulated by the warm and cool air circulating inside them.

The Eastgate Building in Zimbabwe was conceived using this same principle. It's made of several high mounds open at the top in order to regulate the inside temperature. This building has natural air conditioning, so it uses very little energy.

A number of other experiments attempt to bring nature and architecture together. In the United States, in the middle of New Mexico's arid zone, the architect Michael Reynolds is developing what he calls "Earthships." These Earthships are half buried in the ground, and they are eco-friendly and autonomous.

They use the earth's energy to heat themselves
naturally, and they collect rainwater that is then
redistributed to greenhouses where fruit and vegetables
grow. Even in the middle of the desert, these dwellings
are veritable oases, green and lush.

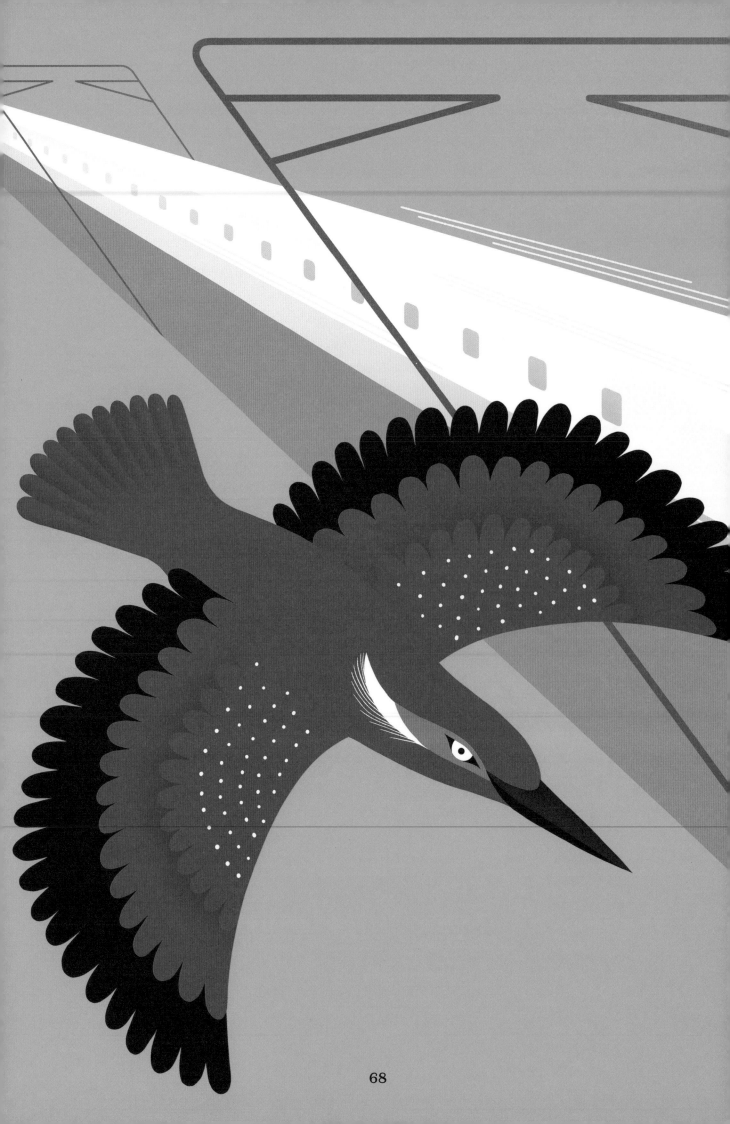

In the area of transportation, design also draws on nature for ideas. The Japanese high-speed train Schinkansen was redesigned to match the morphology of a kingfisher. This new shape made the train faster all while considerably decreasing its energy consumption. It's also the quietest train in the world because its creators were influenced by the owl's silent flight. Owls fly without making a sound.

BIOMIMICRY AND THE FUTURE

As you can see, living creatures develop long-term strategies that we humans can use to create solutions for the future. Observing nature and copying it allows us to move toward more positive and coherent results, in harmony with all of life.

In the future, we may not get holes in our clothes anymore. Our objects will be sturdier, perhaps self-cleaning, with no plastics made from things that pollute our world. Our houses will no doubt become autonomous, regulating their own temperature and producing their own energy. And our organs may be able to cure themselves.

One thing is certain: nature will continue to surprise us and, together, in harmony with nature and with each other, step by step, we will build the world of tomorrow.

So go outside, observe, compare, and maybe someday you'll be the next person to be struck by a great idea.

SÉRAPHINE MENU was born in France, close to the sea, in 1990. After graduating with a degree in literature she wasn't ready to work in an office and decided to travel the world. She visited China, Mexico, and Cuba; and lived in India, the UK, and Canada. During her trips, she met a lot of people and discovered different ways to live. She started to write stories about what she discovered, about herself, about the people and the nature around them. Because a lot of cultures are putting nature at the very heart of their lives, she had the idea to write a book about biomimicry. Now, she lives in Paris, but continues to travel. She has written a novel for teens and has many more projects to come.

EMMANUELLE WALKER is a Swiss/Canadian illustrator with a 2D animation direction and design background. She is the illustrator of *Dogs in Cars and Beautiful Birds*, which was a bestseller and won the prestigious Chen Bochui International Children's Literature awards for best picture book and received an honorary mention for the Opera Prima at the Bologna Book Fair in 2016. She also illustrated *Beautiful Birds Coloring Book* (Flying Eye/Nobrow). Walker lives in London.

ALYSON WATERS translates modern and contemporary literature from the French. In addition to over a dozen books for adults, she has translated four books for children. Her translation of Eric Chevillard's *Prehistoric Times* won the French-American Foundation/Florence Gould prize for best translation from the French in 2013. Her most recent translation is Jean Giono's *A King Alone* (New York Review Books, 2019). She teaches literary translation in the French Department of Yale University, is the managing editor of Yale French Studies, and lives in Brooklyn, New York.

A TRIANGLE SQUARE BOOK FOR YOUNG READERS
PUBLISHED BY SEVEN STORIES PRESS

SEVEN STORIES PRESS
140 Watts Street
New York, NY 10013
www.sevenstories.com

School teachers may order free examination copies
of Seven Stories Press titles.
To order, visit www.sevenstories.com.

LIBRARY OF CONGRESS CATALOGING-IN-PUBLICATION DATA
NAMES: Menu, Séraphine, author. | Walker, Emmanuelle, illustrator.
TITLE: Biomimicry : when nature inspires amazing inventions / Séraphine Menu ; illustrated by Emmanuelle
    Walker ; translated from the French by Alyson Waters.
DESCRIPTION: New York : Seven Stories Press, [2020] | Audience: Grades 4-6
SUMMARY: "Discover how bats led to the development of radar, whales inspired the pacemaker,
    and the lotus flower may help us produce indestructible clothing. "Biomimicry" comes from the Greek
    "bio" (life) and "mimesis" (imitation). Here are various and amazing ways that nature inspires us to create
    cool inventions in science and medicine, clothing design, and architecture. From the fireflies that showed
    inventors how LEDs could give off more light to the burdock plant that inspired velcro to the high speed
    trains of Japan that take the form of a kingfisher's sleek, aerodynamic head, there are innumerable ways
    that we can create smarter, better, safer inventions by observing the natural world. Author Seraphine
    Menu and illustrator Emmanuelle Walker also gently explain that our extraordinary, diverse, and awe-
    inspiring world is like a carefully calibrated machine and its fragile balance must be treated with extreme
    care and respect. "Go outside," they say, "observe, compare, and maybe some
    day you'll be the next person to be struck by a great idea.""—Provided by publisher.
IDENTIFIERS: LCCN 2020009537 (print) | LCCN 2020009538 (ebook) | ISBN 9781644210185
    (hardcover) | ISBN 9781644210208 (ebook)
SUBJECTS: | LCSH: Biomimicry—Juvenile literature. | Technological innovations—Juvenile literature.
CLASSIFICATION: LCC T173.8 .M45413 2020 (print) | LCC T173.8 (ebook) | DDC 620—dc23
LC record available at https://lccn.loc.gov/2020009537
LC ebook record available at https://lccn.loc.gov/2020009538

Printed in China
English edition design by Dror Cohen

9 8 7 6 5 4 3 2 1